Greek Mythology for Kids

Enthralling Greek Myths, Stories, and Legends of Gods, Goddesses, and Mythological Creatures

© **Copyright 2025 - All rights reserved.**

The content contained within this book may not be reproduced, duplicated, or transmitted without direct written permission from the author or the publisher.

Under no circumstances will any blame or legal responsibility be held against the publisher, or author, for any damages, reparation, or monetary loss due to the information contained within this book, either directly or indirectly.

Legal Notice:

This book is copyright protected. It is only for personal use. You cannot amend, distribute, sell, use, quote, or paraphrase any part, or the content within this book, without the consent of the author or publisher.

Disclaimer Notice:

Please note the information contained within this document is for educational and entertainment purposes only. All effort has been executed to present accurate, up-to-date, reliable, and complete information. No warranties of any kind are declared or implied. Readers acknowledge that the author is not engaging in the rendering of legal, financial, medical, or professional advice. The content within this book has been derived from various sources. Please consult a licensed professional before attempting any techniques outlined in this book.

By reading this document, the reader agrees that under no circumstances is the author responsible for any losses, direct or indirect, that are incurred as a result of the use of the information contained within this document, including, but not limited to, errors, omissions, or inaccuracies.

Table of Contents

Introduction 1

Chapter 1: Cosmogony and Theogony 3

Chapter 2: The Olympians, Titans, and Giants 9

Chapter 3: The Creation of Mankind and Other Tales 16

Chapter 4: Heracles and His Labors 24

Chapter 5: Theseus and Athens 38

Chapter 6: Perseus and Andromeda 45

Chapter 7: The Argonauts and the Golden Fleece 51

Chapter 8: The Trojan War 61

Activity Solutions 75

Bibliography 79

Images Sources 80

INTRODUCTION

Ancient people, like us today, tried to figure out where everything came from, what everything was, and how it worked. They told their children many wonderful stories. They spoke of monsters, strange creatures, and shapeshifting gods.

They also told their children real stories of what they and their ancestors had lived through. Those children told their children who would one day tell their children. This continued for generations. Scholars call this way of passing on history and folktales oral history. As you can imagine, retelling history over and over again led it to become mixed up with legends and myths.

In this book, we will introduce you to some Greek myths, legends, and real history. We will see how the gods behaved. The Greeks believed their gods had human emotions, like jealousy, anger, love, and hate. They all had superpowers. Once the gods made humans, these poor creatures were dependent on the whims (moods) of the gods for their well-being. Deities (gods) constantly interfered in their lives.

Come with us as we explore ancient Greek gods whose names and powers were sometimes mixed up in ancient writings. For example, some ancient writers called the underworld (the place where people went when they died) Tartarus (tarr-tarr-uhs). Some called it Erebus (eh-ruh-buhs). And just to confuse the issue a bit more, the Romans took over many of the Greek gods and myths. They gave them different names. The king of the gods, Zeus, became Jupiter. Odysseus (oh-dee-see-us), a famous hero, became Ulysses (you-li-sees).

The most exciting stories were the stories the Greeks made up about how everything worked. The ancient Greeks were very good at this. They even invented myths to explain why good and bad things happened to people. Their stories often have hidden lessons to show people what could happen if they did bad things. We refer to that as "the moral of the story," which means there is a lesson hidden in the story.

A challenge for you

While you are reading or listening to these wonderful stories, try to figure out what the lesson is. What did the ancient Greeks want you to learn from the tale?

Oh, and one more tip for you. You can find the answers to the activities of each chapter at the end of the book.

Chapter 1: Cosmogony and Theogony

We become aware of the world around us when we are just toddlers. We start to wonder and ask our parents and teachers the what, where, how, and why of everything we notice. The ancient people did the same. They made up fascinating stories to explain the wonders of their environment.

Cosmogony (*cos-maa-guh-nee*) is the theories, stories, and ideas of how the universe (the cosmos) came into being. Theogony (*thee-aa-guh-nee*) is the stories and ideas about the deities that live in the universe. To ancient people, everything they could see belonged to one single connected system. The sky, the sun, the moon, the stars, and the earth, with everything above and below the ground, were all part of one large system.

According to Greek mythology, the earth (Gaia) was born out of empty Chaos.[1]

Their gods usually lived in the skies, but some gods lived on the earth. Some of their offspring that populated the earth and skies were gods and *demigods* (half-gods). Some offspring were strange creatures. There were satyrs (*say-ters*), the Hecatoncheires (*he-ka-ton-kee-rees*) with their one hundred arms, one-eyed giants called Cyclopes (*sai-clops*), and other monsters.

Humans lived only on the earth. They were mortals, which means they would die at some point. The gods were immortal, which means they could live forever. Only the half-gods could die like humans. Half gods, also called demigods, were the offspring of a god and a human.

Around 700 BCE, an ancient Greek scholar named Hesiod (*heh-see-uhd*) wrote a long poem called *Theogony* to make sense of the Greek belief system. Hesiod tells how the *Muses* (daughters of Zeus (*zoos*), the king of the gods) told him the stories and names of the gods. They also told him how skills, talents, personality traits, and feelings were given to humans.

Hesiod sorted many Greek myths in an orderly way that started with the beginning. He explained where every god fit into the picture. And there were many gods.

> **Fun Fact**
> People still call somebody who inspires an author or artist their muse.

Each god and goddess had their own mythical story. Authors later added to some of these stories. For example, some ancient accounts say that all water came from a god named Oceanus (*o-shee-a-nuhs*). Others called the source of the salt waters of the seas and oceans Pontus. These people said only the freshwater sources, like rivers, lakes, and springs, came from Oceanus.

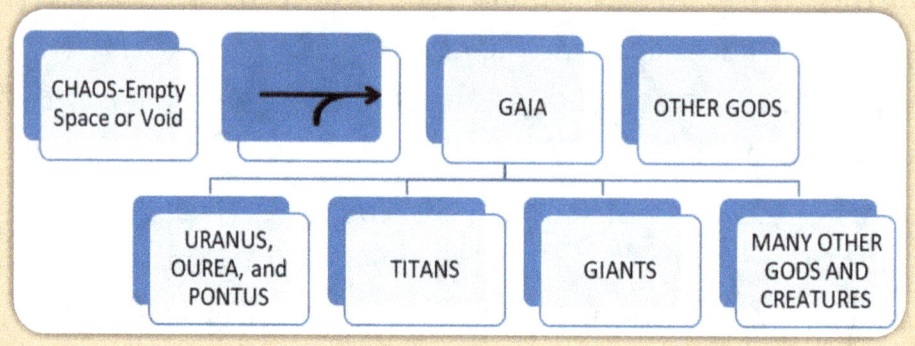

A graph of how the gods came to be. (Created by author)

According to Hesiod, it all began with an empty space called Chaos. Out of Chaos came Gaia (the earth), Tartarus (the underworld), Aether (*ee-ther*) (the light), Nyx (*nix*) (the night), Eros (love), and several more gods and creatures. They were the first deities.

Gaia was the original mother goddess. She produced the heavens (Uranus), the mountains (Ourea), the sea (Pontus), and many other gods. Uranus (*you-ray-nus*) became the king of the gods.

Gaia also produced the next generation of gods. They were called the Titans. Gaia then produced three one-eyed giants and three other horrible creatures.

The giants were known as the Cyclopes. The creatures were called the Hecatoncheires. They had fifty heads and a hundred arms. They represented earthquakes and vicious stormy waves.

Drawing of Gaia.[2]

Uranus hated the Cyclopes and the ugly Hecatoncheires even though he was their father. He hid them away underneath the earth as soon as they were born.

Gaia was sad about her offspring. She made a *sickle* (a big, curved knife) and talked her youngest son, a Titan called Cronos (*crow-nos*), into punishing his father. Cronos cut a piece off his father's body. This removed all his power from him. He would forever stay stuck as the sky above the earth.

As Uranus lay bleeding, he prophesied that Cronos would be destroyed by one of his children.

Statue of Uranus at the Trevi Fountain in Rome.[3]

Gaia had many more offspring. Some of her children were the Gigantes (giants) and the nymphs of the forests, Meliads (*me-ly-ads*).

Chapter 1 Activity

Can you find the words in the word search?

Keywords:

GAIA

GIANTS

OCEANUS

OUREA

CHAOS

URANUS

TARTARUS

NYX

CYCLOPS

PONTUS

HESIOD

T	A	R	T	A	R	U	S	S	Q	Q	Z
X	Y	U	T	E	H	R	G	V	L	I	N
P	M	P	R	U	H	M	I	K	Q	E	B
H	E	B	O	Z	T	N	A	I	J	Z	C
N	U	N	U	X	N	S	N	R	U	L	T
G	J	M	R	C	U	U	T	Z	D	K	Q
V	N	G	E	N	H	E	S	I	O	D	H
U	C	H	A	O	S	U	A	L	B	M	P
R	S	E	X	I	T	A	Q	Z	H	V	I
U	C	T	C	N	A	O	X	Z	W	T	E
O	H	S	O	C	Y	C	L	O	P	S	Y
H	B	P	Q	C	S	X	V	B	F	C	B

Chapter 2: The Olympians, Titans, and Giants

The universe was not yet complete when the Titans became rulers. There were two generations of Titans. For instance, the Titan god Hyperion (*hai-pee-ree-uhn*) was the god of light. Hyperion had three offspring with the Titan goddess of sight, Thea. They were Helios (*he-lee-os*) (the sun), Selene (*se-leen*) (the moon), and Eos (*ee-os*) (the dawn).

The Titans

Cronos came from the first generation of Titans. He became the king of the gods after his father, Uranus, was removed from power. Cronos's wife was a goddess called Rhea (*ray-uh*). She was also a Titan.

Cronos eventually became as evil as his father. He was a cruel and nasty ruler. He swallowed his children as soon as they were born. Cronos was afraid that Uranus's prediction might come true.

When Gaia saw this, she told Rhea to have her next baby far away from Cronos. Rhea listened to the advice and had her baby on the island of Crete. She cleverly wrapped a stone in a blanket afterward and went back to Cronos. When Cronos asked about the baby, she gave him the stone. He stuffed it in his mouth without opening the blanket and swallowed it.

Zeus to the Rescue

Gaia took care of the infant on Crete. After all, he was her grandson. His name was Zeus. When Zeus was strong and old enough, Gaia told him how nasty his father was. He could not remain the king of the gods.

Zeus went to the palace of Cronos and put poison in his father's drink. Cronos became sick and vomited up his children. They had grown into adults inside their father! By the time Cronos felt better, Zeus and his siblings were already back on Crete.

Zeus and his siblings planned to overthrow Cronos. However, Zeus knew that the other Titans would help Cronos. A fight against the mighty Titans would end in defeat for him and his siblings. They needed some help.

A ceiling fresco of the Titanomachy, painted in 1721. It is located in a castle in Germany.[4]

The Titanomachy

Again, it was Gaia who came up with a solution. She advised Zeus to free her other offspring, the Cyclopes and the Hecatoncheires. Uranus had locked them in the underworld. With their help, Zeus and his siblings could surely overcome the Titans. And that is exactly what happened!

The grateful Cyclopes gave Zeus a lightning bolt as a weapon. They gave Hades, Zeus's brother, a helmet that made him invisible when he wore it. Poseidon, another one of Zeus's brothers, received a spear-like weapon with three prongs known as a trident.

Only two of the first-generation Titans joined Zeus's side.

This really big war was called the Titanomachy (*tai-tin-oh-mackee*). It was a hard fight, but Zeus and his siblings won.

Zeus punished most of the Titans by locking them up in Tartarus. Atlas, one of the second-generation Titans who fought with Cronos, was sent to a high mountain to forever hold up the sky on his shoulders.

The Olympians

Zeus and his siblings finally became the next generation of ruling gods. This generation of gods became known as the Olympians. They settled on a high mountain called Mount Olympus in Greece. Zeus was the god of the sky and the earth. He was also the king of all the gods because he rescued his brothers and sisters.

Statue of Zeus.[5]

Zeus's brother Hades (*hay-dees*) became the chief god of the underworld. Another brother named Poseidon (*puh-sai-din*) became the chief god of the oceans.

Zeus had many children. He had some children with Hera, his wife. He had some with Titan goddesses. He even had children with human women. Several of Zeus's children are included in the group known as the Olympians.

Quick Facts about the Olympians

The gods on Olympus are usually referred to as the Twelve Olympians. However, their number and even their names vary. For this list, we used the most popular deities.

- **Zeus** – He was the king and the mightiest of the Olympic gods. He freed his brothers and sisters from their father's stomach. His most well-known symbols were his thunderbolt (lightning) and an eagle.
- **Hera** – She was the queen, wife, and sister of Zeus. She was the goddess of women, childbirth, marriage, and family.
- **Poseidon** – He was the supreme god of all waters. He controlled storms, hurricanes, tsunamis, floods, and droughts. His symbols included his trident, dolphins, horses, and bulls.
- **Athena** – She was the goddess of war, strategy, and defense. She was the daughter of Zeus. She popped out of her father's head fully grown and dressed in battle gear. She was also the goddess of wisdom, knowledge, reason, intelligence, science, literature, and crafts.

- **Apollo** – He was the ideal image of male beauty to the Greeks. He was the god of healing, the sun, light, music, prophesy, and archery. He was the son of Zeus and Leto, a Titan goddess. He had a twin sister named Artemis.

- **Artemis** – She was the daughter of Zeus and Leto. Her twin was Apollo. She was the goddess of hunting, wild animals, flora (plants), purity, women, childbirth, and the moon. She is usually shown with a golden bow and arrows.

- **Aphrodite** – She was the goddess of beauty and love. She was born from the sea foam where Uranus's blood had spattered. She could make people or gods fall in love.

- **Ares** – He was a son of Zeus and Hera. He was the god of war. Ares was admired for his looks and strong warrior skills. However, he was unpopular because he could be cruel.

- **Demeter** – She was Zeus's sister. She was the goddess of the seasons, agriculture, and harvests. Her daughter Persephone was married to Zeus's brother, Hades. Every winter, Demeter is upset that her daughter is in the underworld. That is why plants die in the winter!

- **Hades** – He is not usually considered an Olympian since he did not live on Olympus. He was the god of the underworld. He ruled over everything under the surface of the earth, including humans after they died.

- **Hermes** – He was the messenger of the Olympians. He wore a winged cap and winged sandals that made him very fast. He was the protector of human *heralds* (messengers), travelers, and thieves. He was said to have invented the alphabet and numbers.
- **Hephaestus** – He was Hera's son, but she found him so ugly that she threw him into the sea. He was allowed back on Mount Olympus because he was a skilled metalworker. He made weapons and jewelry for the gods. He was the god of fire and blacksmiths.
- **Hestia** – She was Zeus's sister. She was the eldest child of Cronos and Rhea. She was the goddess of the hearth and home. It is said that she gave up her place as an Olympian and went to live on her own because she was fed up with the gods' constant fighting.
- **Dionysus** – He was the son of Zeus. He was the god of wine, orchards, and fruit. Dionysus became one of the Olympians when Hestia left.

The Olympian deities, with Dionysus lying in the foreground.[6]

Chapter 2 Activity

Circle the correct answer to these multiple-choice questions.

1. **What was the name of the second generation of Greek deities?**
   a) Dorians　　　　b) Lilians　　　　c) Titans

2. **Who was the mother of this second generation?**
   a) Gaia　　　　b) Zelda　　　　c) Rhea

3. **Who became the king of the gods in the second generation?**
   a) Lobos　　　　b) Cronos　　　　c) Calos

4. **What was the name of his wife?**
   a) Lydia　　　　b) Zelda　　　　c) Rhea

5. **What did the king in Question 3 do to his children?**
   a) Swallowed them　　　　b) Praised them
   c) Drowned them.

6. **Where did the queen hide her last baby?**
   a) On Mount Ida　　　　b) In a cave in Italy
   c) On the island of Crete

7. **What was the name of this last baby?**
   a) James　　　　b) Lucas　　　　c) Zeus

8. **What is the battle between the second and third generations of Greek gods called?**
   a) Liberatateo　　　　b) War of the gods
   c) Titanomachy

9. **Who became the king of the Greek gods after the war?**
   a) Helios　　　　b) Hyperion　　　　c) Zeus

10. **Who became the god of the oceans?**
    a) Proteus　　　　b) Poseidon　　　　c) Helios

Chapter 3: The Creation of Mankind and Other Tales

Zeus felt that it was his duty and purpose to fill the earth. He gave two of the Titans who fought on the side of the Olympians in the Titanomachy the task of making humans and animals. These two Titans were named Prometheus (*pro-mee-thee-uhs*) and Epimetheus (*eh-puh-mee-thee-uhs*). To help them, Zeus gave them all sorts of gifts they could bestow on their creations.

The First Humans

Prometheus made humans from mud. He made them in the shape of the gods, but he made only men. One of Zeus's children, Athena, gave the clay humans breath so they could be alive.

Epimetheus was happily making animals. He did not plan ahead. He generously gave them all of Zeus's gifts for survival.

Prometheus was very intelligent. He took his time planning ahead. He wanted to make the perfect human.

Since Epimetheus had used up all the useful gifts, Prometheus had to think of something to help his creations. To help the weak and defenseless humans, Prometheus made them stand upright so they could see far and wide. He taught them many practical skills to make useful things like plows, clothes, and weapons. He also gave them intelligence and taught them astronomy, mathematics, and other sciences. Then, he stole fire from the gods.

Prometheus bringing stolen fire to the humans.[7]

Prometheus and the Revenge of Zeus

Prometheus loved his creation so much that he made more humans. The Olympians watched this from their thrones on Mount Olympus. They decided the humans owed them a portion of what they made. They could not decide what this portion should be. To settle the matter, the gods and humans held a great feast. Prometheus sacrificed an ox. Zeus then had to choose between two sacks of cooked meat.

Prometheus knew the gods would want the best pieces of meat. He did not agree because he felt his hardworking creations should get the best meat. He tricked Zeus by filling one sack with bones and putting just a few pieces of tasty meat and fat on top. The other sack was full of the best meat, but that meat was covered with skin and tough meat. Zeus chose the sack with the bones.

Zeus was angry and punished the humans by taking away their fire. Prometheus knew humans depended on fire for light, warmth, and cooking. He stole fire for the humans and hid it in a small tube.

When Zeus found out, he punished Prometheus. Prometheus was chained naked to a rock. Every day, a great eagle would eat his liver, and every night, it would grow back. Heracles would one day kill the eagle and free Prometheus.

Pandora: The First Woman

Zeus was still angry with the humans for all the skills and gifts Prometheus had given them. He instructed the blacksmith god Hephaestus (*huh-fay-stuhs*) to make a very beautiful human out of clay. This was to be the first woman.

Each of the Olympians gave her a gift. She was given beautiful clothes, a crown of flowers, speech, charm, skills like weaving, and everything a man could possibly want in a companion. The gods named her Pandora, which means "all gifted."

Remember, Zeus wanted to punish mankind with this gift. So, the gods also gave her a stubborn, curious, shameless, deceitful nature. She was given a lying tongue that could cause deep hurt and pain.

Pandora's Jar

Before Zeus sent Pandora to marry Epimetheus, the gods gave her a jar. They said this jar was filled with gifts. However, they warned her never to open it.

Epimetheus had been warned by Prometheus never to accept anything from Zeus. But when Epimetheus saw Pandora, he could not resist her beauty and married her.

Out of curiosity, Pandora opened the jar one day. Out flew all the evils and hardships that could affect humans. There was sickness, jealousy, cruelty, greed, hatred, and much more. Pandora was so frightened that she immediately tried to close the lid. It was too late. Only hope did not escape the jar.

Pandora with her jar of evil gifts. [8]

Fun Fact

" Since the 15th century CE, authors have been calling the jar a "box" because one translator incorrectly translated the word Hesiod used. "

The Flood

The people became greedy and evil as time went on. Prometheus had a son called Deucalion (*due-ka-lee-on*). He married Epimetheus and Pandora's daughter. Her name was Pyrrha (*perr-hah*). Deucalion and Pyrrha were considered the most righteous humans.

When Zeus and the other gods decided to destroy the humans because they were so bad, Deucalion pleaded with Zeus to spare them. Zeus refused because his mind was made up after he saw a man sacrificing a child.

Zeus planned to send a great flood to destroy all the wicked people. Deucalion's father, Prometheus, advised him to build a boat to save himself and Pyrrha. Rain and storms beat down upon the earth for nine days and nights until all the earth was covered. Deucalion and Pyrrha sailed the mighty waters in their little boat. They cried when they saw the terrible devastation left by the flood when they were on land again.

A New Generation of Humans

Deucalion and Pyrrha realized they were all that was left. They wanted to fill the earth with people but did not know how. They asked Themis, a goddess on Mount Olympus, for advice. She told them to throw stones over their shoulders without looking back. They were puzzled but followed her advice.

Deucalion and Pyrrha throwing stones over their shoulders. [9]

They were surprised to see the stones turn into men and women. And so, the earth was repopulated.

You may be wondering what happened to the animals. Well, according to some ancient myths, new animals were born from the ground!

Chapter 3 Activity

Can you solve the crossword below?

CLUES:

ACROSS

2 Which bird ate a part of Prometheus every day?

4 What part of Prometheus was eaten every day?

DOWN

1 How did Zeus destroy the first humans?

3 Who made humans breathe?

6. Who made the first humans?

10. Prometheus made only one gender of humans. Which one?

11. What did Deucalion and Pyrrha throw to make new people?

13. In what did Deucalion and Pyrrha survive the flood?

14. What did Zeus want to do to the humans when they became bad?

5. What was the first human made of?

6. The name of the first woman made by Hephaestus.

7. What did Prometheus cook at the feast for the gods and humans?

8. What was left in Pandora's jar when she closed the lid?

9. What did the humans and gods do together in this chapter?

12. What did Prometheus steal from the gods for the humans?

Chapter 4: Heracles and His Labors

Zeus's chief wife was also the queen of the gods. Her name was Hera. She was very jealous, but she had good reason to be. Zeus often fell in love with other women. Hera did not try to punish the mighty Zeus. Instead, she took revenge on the poor women that Zeus fell in love with!

Zeus had a baby with a very beautiful human princess named Alcmene (*al-ke-mee-nee*). This baby was named Heracles. Hera hated the baby as much as she hated his mother. She put snakes in his crib when he was only seven days old. However, the strong, healthy infant strangled the snakes. Hera hated him even more after that. She would pester him all his life.

> **FUN FACT**
> The Romans told tales of Heracles. They called him Hercules.

Heracles strangling the snakes.[10]

The Age of Heroes

The ancient Greek authors named the *era* (period) in which Heracles lived the Age of Heroes. The ancient Greeks believed the heroes and their deeds were based on real stories.

When Heracles grew up, he got married. Hera was still seeking revenge. She cursed him with madness. Heracles did not know what he was doing and killed his wife and children. When he came to his senses, he was devastated about what he had done.

Heracles asked the *seer* (oracle or prophetess) of Delphi what he should do to *atone* (make amends or make right) for the terrible deed. The oracle acted as the spokesperson for the god Apollo. She told him that he must work for King Eurystheus (*you-rees-sthee-us*) for twelve years and complete every task the king gave him.

King Eurystheus gave Heracles ten dangerous tasks to complete. Heracles's labors differ depending on the source. Writers added more deeds and adventures to the legends of Heracles. This makes sense. He was the most famous and popular of the Greek heroes.

Let's take a look at the Labors of Heracles.

- **Killing the Nemean Lion** – This *invincible* (unbeatable) man-eating lion was a threat to the people and farm animals of Nemea. No hunter could kill it. Their spears and arrows could not get through the lion's skin.

  Heracles discovered that its golden fur was made of metal. He blocked one of the lion's entrances to its den. Heracles went in the only other entrance. Once inside, he strangled the beast with his bare hands.

King Eurystheus had ordered Heracles to bring him the skin of the lion. Heracles found it impossible to remove. The goddess Athena came to his aid. She told him the only way to remove it was to use the lion's own claws.

- **Killing the Hydra** — The Hydra was a terrifying monster with nine heads. It lived in the swamps of Lerna. The Hydra caught and ate the people's farm animals.

Chopping off the main head caused the monster to die. Chopping off any of the other heads caused it to grow two heads in its place. Heracles made a plan.

Heracles wearing the skin of the Nemean lion and Iolaus with his torch, killing the Hydra.[11]

He took his nephew, Iolaus, with him. As soon as Heracles chopped a head off, Iolaus set fire to the stump. After eight of the heads had been cut off,

Heracles was able to chop off the main head without any other heads snapping and biting at him.

Just to make sure the monster was completely dead, Heracles buried the last head and placed a large stone on top. Then, he cut the Hydra open and dipped his arrows in its poisonous blood. From then on, his arrows would be deadly.

- **Catching the Ceryneian Hind** – This task was a tricky one. The animal belonged to the goddess of the hunt, Artemis. Imagine having to catch a *fleet-footed* (fast) deer! The beautiful *doe* (female deer) had golden horns and bronze hoofs. It stood taller than a bull.

  Heracles was ready to give up after trying to capture it for a year. Then, he decided to just wound the animal. Artemis was angry, but she forgave him after Heracles explained what was going on. He was able to take the deer to King Eurystheus. He later gave it back to Artemis.

- **The Erymanthian Boar** – This animal was an angry, destructive, and large wild pig with big tusks. The Erymanthian (*ery-man-thian*) boar killed humans and animals. It also destroyed crops.

  The king ordered Heracles to bring the animal to him alive. Heracles screamed and shouted at the boar. Then, he stomped toward it. The boar was shocked! Everything usually ran away from him as fast as it could. So, the boar turned and ran.

  Heracles chased after it. They ran around the mountain until the boar was too tired to go on. It found a clump of bushes and tried to hide. Heracles poked around with his spear until the boar fled. It ran straight into a thick pile of snow. Heracles trapped him in a net and carried him back to King Eurystheus.

The king was scared of Heracles by now. He could not believe that Heracles had lived and succeeded at all these impossible tasks. Heracles had proved his strength and courage over and over again. What task could he give Heracles that would defeat his courage? Maybe working in disgusting filth would be too much for him to bear?

- **The Augean Stables** – King Augeas (*ay-gas*) was a very rich king in ancient Greece. He loved his animals, especially his cattle. To protect these animals from danger, they were brought home from the pastures every evening to sleep safely in an enormous stable.

The stables had not been cleaned for thirty years. It must have stunk something awful! King Eurystheus ordered Heracles to clean the stables. He gave him just one day to do this.

Without telling King Augeas about King Eurystheus's order, Heracles offered to clean the stables if King Augeas would give him one-tenth of his cattle. The king agreed. Heracles took the king's son with him as a witness. He watched as Heracles made large holes on opposite sides of the walls.

The stable was near two rivers. The clever Heracles dug deep trenches between the rivers and the stable. Then, he diverted the rivers to flow through one of the holes in the wall. The water went through the stable and out the opposite hole to the other river.

The rushing waters got into every nook and cranny. All the filth and dirt went into the river. The stables were finally clean.

- **The Stymphalian Birds** – The Stymphalian (*stim-fay-lian*) birds were vicious flesh-eating birds. They could shoot their bronze feathers out of their skin like arrows. The birds lived in a forest surrounding a lake in Stymphalos. They ate the crops and attacked humans who came near them.

  Chasing these birds away was Heracles's next task. He had no idea how he was going to do it. There were just too many birds. They were spread all over the forest and the lake.

  The goddess Athena came to Heracles's aid. She brought him a special pair of bronze clappers that made a loud clicking noise. Heracles stood on a high mountain close to the forest and clicked these instruments. They made a terrible noise that scared the birds from their nests. Heracles shot many of them down with his arrows. He continued making this terrible noise until all the birds were dead or had flown away.

- **The Cretan Bull** – On the island of Crete, there was a beautiful white bull with a very bad temper. Eurystheus decided he wanted this bull. So, this became Heracles's next task.

Heracles, with his Nemean lion hood and cloak, catching the Cretan bull.[12]

Heracles got to work. This time, he only needed his great strength. He fought the bull until it was too tired to get up. Heracles slung it over his shoulders and carried it to King Eurystheus. He set the bull free after the king saw it.

Fun Fact

> Many myths about this bull circulated in Greece and beyond. It supposedly roamed all over Greece and wreaked havoc wherever it went. Another Greek hero, Theseus (thee-see-uhs), killed it at Marathon.

- **The Horses of Diomedes** – Across the sea lived a king called Diomedes (*dy-oh-mee-dees*). He was one of the giants. He had four beautiful mares to pull his chariot. This terrible giant fed his horses human flesh, which made them crazy.

  In some versions of this myth, Heracles had to bring back the horses and the chariot. He took a few young men with him for this task. They overcame the giants and stole the horses. However, Diomedes and his men came after them.

  Heracles left his friend, Abderos (*ab-dee-ros*), to take care of the horses while he went after Diomedes. Heracles killed the giants. When he got back to the horses, he discovered they had eaten Abderos. Heracles fed them the flesh of Diomedes, which calmed them down. Then, he took them to King Eurystheus.

  In some myths, the king sacrificed the horses to Hera. In other versions, Heracles set them free after he showed them to Eurystheus. They wandered off toward Mount Olympus, where wild animals ate them.

- **The Belt of Hippolyte** – Hippolyte (*hi-poll-i-tee*) was the queen of the Amazons. The Amazons were a tribe of fierce warrior women who lived across the sea. Eurystheus's daughter heard that Hippolyte had a *girdle* (belt) given to her by Ares (*air-ees*), the god of war. She wanted the girdle, so Eurystheus decided that would be Heracles's next task.

Hippolyte had heard of Heracles and all his mighty deeds. She welcomed him. When Heracles told her the reason for his visit, she promised to give him her belt. He invited her to have lunch with him on his ship.

In the meantime, Hera disguised herself as an Amazon. She said the men on the ship were planning to abduct the queen. The Amazons grew upset. They armed themselves, jumped on their horses, and raced to the harbor.

Heracles thought that Hippolyte had plotted an attack behind his back. He killed her and took her belt.

Some stories say there was a lot of fighting between the Amazons and the Greeks. Others say that Heracles and his crew sailed away as soon as he got the belt.

- **Geryon's Cattle** – A monstrous giant named Geryon (*jee-ree-uhn*) lived on an island at the edge of the world. Geryon had a valuable herd of red oxen. The oxen were stained red by the setting sun.

Geryon had a vicious two-headed dog and a giant to guard his oxen. King Eurystheus wanted this herd of oxen, so he made that Heracles's next task.

Heracles and his crew sailed to the far west. On the way, they had many adventures. At one point, Heracles became really angry because it was so hot. He shot an arrow at Helios, the sun god, who was traveling across the sky. Instead of being angry, Helios was impressed. He rewarded Heracles by lending him his golden ship. Heracles and his crew arrived at Geryon's island in just one night!

Heracles and his men quickly found the herd of red oxen, but the dog monster tackled them. Heracles killed him with one blow of his club. Then, the giant tried to stop them. Heracles also killed him with his club.

The Greeks herded the oxen to the harbor. As soon as Geryon heard what was happening, he grabbed his shield and weapons and stormed after the thieves. Heracles shot an arrow into his forehead, killing the giant.

Heracles delivered the oxen to Eurystheus, who sacrificed them to Hera.

This should have been the end of Heracles's labors. However, Eurystheus added two extra labors. He said Heracles could not count the labors where he had extra help.

- **The Apples of the Hesperides** —Eurystheus ordered Heracles to steal the golden apples from the Hesperides (*hi-sperr-i-dees*). Heracles did not even know where to look for them. He traveled throughout Greece and other lands.

  At last, he heard from the water nymphs how he could get the location from their father, Nereus (*neh-roos*). Nereus was a Titan. He told Heracles how to get to the gardens.

The Hesperides.[13]

Fun Fact

" Homer called Nereus the "Old Man of the Sea." Nereus is in the third book of the Percy Jackson series. "

Do you recall the terrible punishment that Zeus gave Prometheus for stealing fire? Well, poor Prometheus had seen several generations of humans come and go. Yet, he was still chained to the rock. Heracles shot and killed the eagle. Then, with his bare hands, he broke the chains that bound Prometheus.

Prometheus told Heracles the exact place where the Hesperides lived. He warned him not to pick the apples himself. Instead, he should ask their father, Atlas, to pick the apples. Atlas could go into the garden without fearing the vicious dragon that guarded the apples.

But Atlas held up the sky. How could Heracles make Atlas leave his post?

Heracles offered to hold the sky up for Atlas so that he could stretch his muscles and pick some apples. Atlas agreed. When Atlas returned, he refused to exchange places. The sky was heavy, and Atlas did not want to hold it anymore.

The *wily* (clever) Heracles acted as though he agreed. He asked Atlas just one favor. Atlas needed to hold the sky for a moment so that Heracles could adjust his cloak to protect his shoulders. As soon as Atlas took up the weight of the sky, Heracles grabbed the apples and left.

When Heracles arrived back at the court of King Eurystheus, the king told him to keep the apples for himself. Heracles gifted the apples to Athena. She gave them back to the Hesperides.

- **Cerberus** – One more deadly task awaited Heracles. King Eurystheus sent him to fetch Cerberus (*sir-bur-oos*). Cerberus was a deadly three-headed dog who guarded the entrance to the underworld. Cerberus had a snake for a tail. He belonged to Hades, the god of the underworld.

Heracles eventually arrived at the throne of Hades. He told the god about his quest. Hades gave Heracles permission to take Cerberus as long as he did not use any weapons.

Heracles wrestled the dog to the ground using his bare hands. Then, he took it back to the land of the living. When he presented it to Eurystheus, the king was so overwhelmed by the sight of the hideous monster that he hid. He told Heracles to take the dog back to Hades.

At last, Heracles's labors were over. Heracles would still have many more adventures. In the end, his father, Zeus, gave him a place in Olympus as one of the gods.

Chapter 4 Activity

Circle the correct answer to the following multiple-choice questions.

1. **Heracles was a _____**
   a. Giant	b. Human	c. Demigod

2. **Heracles was the son of which god?**
   a. Hades	b. Poseidon	c. Zeus

3. **Who put snakes in Heracles's crib?**
   a. Athena	b. Artemis	c. Hera

4. **Hera drove Heracles insane, and he killed his wife and children. How many labors did he have to complete to atone for the murders?**
   a. Eight	b. Twelve	c. Fifteen

5. **What kind of animal terrorized the Nemeans?**
   a. Snake	b. Giant Dog	c. Lion

6. **How many heads did the Hydra have?**
   a. Five	b. Seven	c. Nine

7. **What was the color of the Cretan bull?**
   a. Purple	b. Red	c. White

8. **What did Heracles use to clean the filthy stables of King Augeas?**
   a. Broom	b. Vacuum Cleaner	c. Rivers

9. **What kind of animal was Cerberus?**
   a. Wolf	b. Brown Bear	c. Dog

10. **What weapon did Heracles use to kill the giant Geryon?**
    a. Sword	b. Slingshot	c. Arrow

Chapter 5: Theseus and Athens

Thucydides (*thoo-si-duh-dees*), an ancient historian, believed Theseus was a real person. Scholars today still do not agree on who was real and who was mythical. It is sort of like Batman, Spiderman, and Superman mixed into stories of Paul Revere, Christopher Columbus, and Abraham Lincoln!

Theseus was the son of Aegeus, the king of Athens, and Aethra (*ath-ra*), a princess of Troezen (*Tro-e-zin*). Some say his real father was Poseidon, the god of the oceans.

Theseus grew up with his mother in Troezen. When Theseus was a young man, his mother gave him his father's sword and sandals. Aegeus told Aethra that if she had a boy, she was to give him the sword and sandals. She was also supposed to send him to Athens when he grew up. That way, Aegeus would recognize his son.

Theseus finding his father's sandals.[14]

The City of Athens

Once Theseus grew up, he traveled to Athens. The first person to recognize Theseus was the wicked sorceress Medea (*muh-dee-ah*). She was married to Aegeus. Medea knew she had to get rid of Theseus before his father saw him and recognized the sandals and sword!

She tricked King Aegeus into demanding that the stranger kill the wild bull at Marathon. This was the same mad bull that Heracles had caught for King Eurystheus.

Theseus managed to catch the bull. He showed it to the king and queen. He then sacrificed it to the god Apollo.

Next, Medea tried to poison Theseus. Aegeus finally recognized his sword and sandals just before the young man drank what Medea had given him. Aegeus smacked it out of his hand. The king realized what Medea had tried to do, and he banished her from Athens.

The Minotaur

King Minos of Crete demanded *retribution* (revenge). Seven young women and seven young men had to be sent to Crete every seventh year. They were fed to the Minotaur (*mi-nuh-tor*), a monstrous half-bull and half-man creature that lived in a *labyrinth* (maze) on Crete.

When Theseus heard about this, he resolved to be part of the next group. King Aegeus pleaded with Theseus, but his mind was made up. He wanted to kill the bull and save the young people of Athens.

The ship that carried the youths to Crete always had black sails. Theseus promised his father that he would replace them with white sails on his way back so that the king would know if he was alive.

Theseus fighting the Minotaur.[15]

Ariadne Helps Theseus

King Minos had a beautiful daughter named Ariadne (*eh-ree-ad-nee*). She fell instantly in love with Theseus. Ariadne gave him a ball of twine and instructions on how to find the Minotaur. She got all this information from the builder of the labyrinth, Daedalus (*deh-duh-luhs*).

The Athenians were sent into the labyrinth. Theseus told them to let him go first. He tied the string to the entrance and unrolled it as he went along. He went into the deepest parts of the labyrinth, where he found the Minotaur.

Theseus had managed to hide his sword under his clothes when the Cretans took the Athenian youths' weapons. After a huge fight, he managed to kill the beast. He then followed the string out of the labyrinth.

Theseus exits the labyrinth after killing the Minotaur.[16]

The Athenians fled on their ship. They took Ariadne with them. Theseus had promised to marry her. They stopped at the island of Naxos to celebrate their victory.

For some reason, Ariadne was not with them when they left Naxos. Ancient writers told different stories of why this happened. Some say Theseus left her behind because he did not love her. Another story says the god of wine, Dionysus (*dai-uh-nai-suhs*), wanted her for himself. He took her to Mount Olympus, where she became his immortal wife.

Theseus forgot to replace the black sails of his ship with white ones. King Aegeus was anxiously watching from the cliffs at Cape Sounion high above the sea. When he saw the black sails, he was so devastated that he threw himself off the cliff. Theseus was now the king of Athens.

> **Fun Fact**
> Many ancient Greek and Roman authors wrote stories about Theseus. We do not know when most of these stories fit into the lifespan of Theseus.

He married several women. Phaedra (*fay-druh*), a daughter of King Minos of Crete, married Theseus. She fell in love with Hippolytus (*huh-paa-luh-tuhs*), her stepson, while she was married to Theseus. Hippolytus was the son of Theseus and Hippolyta, the Amazon queen. When Hippolytus rejected Phaedra, she told the king that Theseus had attacked her. Theseus cursed his son and caused his death. Phaedra committed suicide out of guilt.

Theseus's Spirit Fights On

Theseus was once stuck in the underworld for months. He wasn't even dead!

Theseus and his best friend Pirithous (*pee-ree-sthous*) wanted more wives. They went to the underworld to abduct Persephone (*per-seh-fuh-nee*). Persephone was married to Hades, the chief god of the underworld.

Theseus and Pirithous grew tired and sat down to rest. When they tried to get up, they found they were cemented to the chairs! Heracles eventually freed Theseus when he went to the underworld to catch Cerberus.

Theseus discovered that another king was on the throne in Athens. He fled to an island, where the king threw him off a cliff. Many years later, during the wars between the Persians and Greeks, soldiers swore they saw the ghost of Theseus fighting with them. They searched for his bones and reburied them in Athens. A great temple was built over his tomb.

Chapter 5 Activity

Can you help Theseus find the Minotaur in the center of this labyrinth?

Chapter 6: Perseus and Andromeda

Perseus (*pur-see-uhs*) was a demigod. His father was Zeus. His mother was a *mortal* (human) princess called Danae (*da-nuh-ee*).

Danae's father put her and baby Perseus in a chest and launched them into the sea. He wanted to send them as far away as possible. He believed in a prophecy that Danae's child would one day kill him.

The chest bobbed and weaved through the *turbulent* (wild) waves. Danae held Perseus tightly in her arms. Zeus made sure the chest landed on an island.

The brother of the king of that island found them. He was a fisherman named Dictys (*dik-tees*). He was a kind and gentle man. He offered them his home and looked after them for years. Perseus grew up under the guidance of this kind fisherman.

Danae and baby Perseus are saved by Dictys.[17]

One day, many years later, the king, Polydectes (*poly-dek-tees*), visited his brother. He saw the beautiful Danae. Polydectes wanted her for himself. He took her to his palace and tried to win her love. But Danae rejected him.

Polydectes became frustrated. He thought he could force her to marry him. However, there was a problem. He knew that her strong son would not allow that.

Perseus and Medusa

So, Polydectes sent Perseus on a quest to find and kill Medusa (*muh-doo-sah*) and bring him her head.

Medusa had been a priestess in the temple of Athena. She was the most beautiful and purest of all the priestesses. Poseidon, the god of the sea, saw her. He was so smitten with the beautiful maiden that he even followed her into the temple of Athena. Athena's temple was sacred. Only innocent women were allowed in there.

Athena could not punish the mighty Poseidon. So, she blamed Madusa for her beauty and charm. Athena's turned Medusa's beautiful hair into a bunch of hissing, writhing snakes. She also put a curse on Medusa. Anybody who looked at her would immediately be turned to stone.

Medusa and her two ugly sisters were known as the Gorgons. They lived in a secret place where they could hide from people.

Perseus did not know where the Gorgons lived. However, Athena had a soft spot for Perseus. She sent him to the Graeae (*gray-ee*). They were three toothless, blind, old women who shared one eye and one tooth between the three of them.

Perseus tricked the Graeae into revealing the way to the nymphs who knew where the Gorgons were. The helpful nymphs told him where to find the Gorgons. They also gave him a pair of winged sandals, a thick bag, and the magic helmet of Hades. This helmet made the wearer invisible. Athena gave him her shield to use as a mirror. Hermes (*her-mees*) gave him a sharp sickle to chop off Medusa's head with one stroke.

Perseus found the Gorgons asleep. He walked backward, using the shield as a mirror to guide him. He chopped off Medusa's head without looking directly at her.

Out of Medusa's neck sprang a beautiful horse with wings called Pegasus (*peh-guh-suhs*) and a golden sword.

Perseus with the head of Medusa.[18]

Perseus quickly popped the head into the bag. He flew away on Pegasus. The other two Gorgons chased him in vain.

Perseus later gave the head to Athena as a gift. Athena made it part of her shield.

A Good Deed for Atlas

Perseus had many more adventures on his way back to his home. When he flew past poor Atlas, he changed him into a rocky outcrop. This saved the Titan from the pain and discomfort he felt every day. The mountain range in the north of Africa is still called the Atlas Mountains.

Andromeda

Perseus eventually came to Aethiopia (*Ee-tee-o-pia*), a part of Sudan today. The king of this country was waiting for the horrible sea monster Cetus (*see-tis*) to take his beloved daughter Andromeda (*an-draa-muh-duh*). Andromeda was chained to a rock in the sea. She was being offered to Cetus to calm the stormy seas that were destroying Aethiopia's coastline and people.

Andromeda's mother, Cassiopeia (*kas-ee-uh-pee-uh*), had offended the gods by bragging that she was more beautiful than the Nereids (*nee-ree-uhdz*). They were the nymphs of the sea and daughters of the gods. Surely, everybody of that time knew that one should never offend a god or goddess! But Cassiopeia apparently did not.

Andromeda was beautiful. Perseus fell in love with her as soon as he saw her. He made a deal with the king that he would slay the monster if Andromeda could become his bride. Perseus flew over the terrible monster. He showed it

Medusa's head. The monster turned into stone, and Andromeda was saved. The king was so happy, and the couple got married.

Perseus fights Cetus to save Andromeda.[19]

Death of Perseus

When Perseus returned home, his mother was hiding in a temple to avoid King Polydectes. Perseus used Medusa's head to turn the king and his *courtiers* (attendants) into stone. Then, he made Dictys the king of the island.

After more adventures, Perseus founded Mycenae (*mai-see-nee*). He ruled the city for a long time. He was a very good leader.

When Perseus died, he was rewarded for his selfless life by becoming a constellation in the sky. Andromeda also became a constellation. Andromeda is near the Perseus constellation.

Chapter 6 Activity

Unscramble the letters to discover the names of people from the story of Perseus. You can use the last column to write your answers!

	CLUES	Scrambled Name	Unscrambled Name
1	Wife of Perseus	OMDRANEDA	A
2	Mother-in-law of Perseus	SIOPCASEIA	C
3	Titan holding up the sky	LASTA	A
4	Flesh-eating sea monster	CESUT	C
5	This goddess gave Perseus her shield	AHENTA	A
6	She had snakes instead of hair on her head	SADUME	M
7	No. 6 and her ugly sisters were known as …	GNOORGS	G
8	This fisherman raised Perseus	YCTIDS	D
9	Perseus's mother's name	AENAD	D
10	The winged horse in the story	GAPESUS	P

Chapter 7: The Argonauts and the Golden Fleece

Jason was a descendant of Hermes through his mother. His father was King Aeson (*ay-son*) of Iolcus (*eye-ole-cuss*). Pelias (*pee-lee-uhs*), the king's half-brother, was a traitor who illegally seized the throne. He imprisoned the rightful king in a dungeon and got rid of anyone who could challenge his kingship.

When Jason was born, his mother and her servants cried. They held a mock funeral to trick Pelias into thinking the baby was dead. Jason's mother smuggled him away. She left him with a wise centaur, Chiron (*kai-ruhn*), in the mountains.

Chiron was a trainer of kings and heroes. He taught Jason all the skills and knowledge needed to become a brave and educated man.

Jason's Quest

When Jason was twenty years old, he went back to Iolcus to claim his throne. King Pelias was warned by an oracle that he must be wary of a young man arriving in the city with only one sandal.

Now, it just so happened that Jason helped an old woman cross a river on his way to Iolcus. He did not know, but the old woman was actually Hera in disguise. He lost a sandal in the river, so he arrived in the city with one bare foot. This allowed Pelias to recognize Jason.

When Jason demanded the kingdom from him, Pelias said he could have it. However, there was a condition. Jason first had to bring him the Golden Fleece. Jason agreed. He gathered a group of brave young men to go with him.

The men set sail on a large ship named the *Argo*. The group soon became known as

Fun Fact: Heracles and Theseus were Argonauts.

the Argonauts. The ancient Greeks believed this was the first long voyage ever undertaken by Greek sailors.

The Golden Fleece

In a sacred grove near the city of Colchis (*kowl-kuhs*) hung a treasured sheepskin with golden wool. It was known as the Golden Fleece. It was fiercely guarded by a dragon.

The fleece came from a winged ram who saved the children of a king after he left them and their mother for another woman. The ram flew the children to a safe place on the opposite side of the Black Sea. While flying over the sea, the girl slipped off and drowned.

Her brother sacrificed the ram to Zeus when he arrived safely in Colchis. He gave the skin to the king of that land. The ram became the constellation of Aries.

The Trip to Colchis

The voyage to Colchis was very long. The Argonauts had to stop several times on the way. If you look at a map of

Greece and its surroundings, you will see that the country has many islands.

The Argonauts stopped on the island of Lemnos. Only women lived on this island. The women had neglected to honor the Olympian goddess of beauty and love, Aphrodite. She cursed them with a foul smell that made the men vomit when they came near them. The women were angry and killed the men.

The Argonauts thought they smelled lovely. They stayed with the women for weeks. Some even got married! Heracles eventually got Jason to gather his men and board the ship again.

The Argonauts on the Argo. [22]

Their next stop was at the port city of the friendly Doliones (*daw-lee-ons*). Jason and most of the Argonauts went to search for food in the countryside. Only Heracles and a few men stayed behind to guard the *Argo*.

The land was also home to a vicious race of six-armed giants. They attacked the ship. Heracles managed to hold them back until the rest of the crew arrived. Together, they fought off the giants and quickly set sail.

During the night, a strong wind blew the ship back to shore. The friendly Doliones did not recognize the ship in the darkness. They thought they were being attacked. The Argonauts also did not realize they had been blown back to the same place.

The two sides started fighting each other. In the morning, both sides realized what had happened. They held a large funeral for the dead. They forgave each other, and the Argonauts resumed their journey.

Jason and the Argonauts next made landfall in the land of King Phineus (*fin-ee-us*). The king was blind and starving because the Harpies terrorized him. The Harpies were evil birds with the faces of humans. They ate and pooped in the king's food every day.

When the king told Jason his sad story, the Argonauts scared the Harpies away for good. King Phineas was a seer. He was able to tell Jason where the Golden Fleece was. He also advised the crew on how to overcome the next obstacle on their journey.

The *Argo* had to sail through a narrow passage between two rocky cliffs, the Symplegades (*sim-pleg-uh-deez*), to reach

Colchis. These cliffs could move by themselves. Every time a vessel tried to sail through, they would come together and smash the ship to pieces.

King Phineus told Jason that he should send a dove through the passage while the *Argo* waited at the entrance. The fast-flying dove would escape before the cliffs crashed into each other. When the cliffs started moving apart, the *Argo* should quickly slip through. The Argonauts followed Phineas's advice and got through safely.

Jason's Challenges

At last, the Argonauts arrived at Colchis. King Aeetes (*a-ee-tees* or *ee-tees*) gave Jason three impossible tasks to complete. If Jason could complete them, Aeetes promised to give him the fleece.

Hera, the queen of the gods, came to Jason's aid. She got Eros to shoot the king's daughter, Medea, with a tiny magic arrow. This made Medea fall in love with Jason.

You may remember Medea from our story about Theseus. She was a sorceress. Medea wanted to protect her love. She helped Jason to complete the tasks.

- Jason had to plow a field with two bulls that breathed fire. Medea gave him magic ointment that stopped the flames from burning him. He quickly plowed the field.
- Jason had to plant the field with dragon's teeth. These magic teeth sprouted into an army of soldiers that would attack Jason. Jason followed Medea's advice again. He threw a rock in the middle of the group of soldiers. They did not see where the rock came from and started fighting each other.

- Jason had to get past the vicious dragon that never slept, fetch the fleece, and bring it to King Aeetes.

Jason with the Golden Fleece. [23]

King Aeetes had already planned to attack and kill Jason and his Argonauts after the third task. Medea was one step ahead. She suspected what her father was planning. She fled the palace and led Jason to the grove where the Golden Fleece was kept. She fed the dragon a powerful sleeping potion. Jason quickly grabbed the fleece after it fell asleep. Jason, Medea, and the Argonauts boarded the *Argo* to sail back to Iolcus.

Victory Turned to Tragedy

The Argonauts overcame several more obstacles on their way back. They eventually arrived in Iolcus.

Jason expected to finally take the throne from King Pelias, just as he had been promised. But Pelias, who had stolen the throne from Jason's father years ago, refused to give up his power. This made Jason and his new wife, Medea, very angry.

Medea came up with a trick to get rid of the wicked king. She told Pelias's daughters that she knew a special magic spell that could make an old person young again. To prove it worked, she took an old, weak *ram* (a type of sheep), cut it into pieces, and placed them in a boiling cauldron filled with a secret potion. Then, with her magic, she made a young, strong lamb jump out of the pot!

Pelias's daughters were amazed. They thought Medea could do the same for their father. So, they cut their father into pieces and put him into the boiling pot.

But Medea had tricked them. She never added the magic potion this time. Pelias was dead, and he would not be coming back.

With the wicked king gone, Jason should have been able to take the throne, but the people of Iolcus were horrified by what had happened. They banished Jason and Medea from the city.

Jason and Medea traveled to Corinth, where they hoped to start fresh and build a new life. For a while, things seemed peaceful. They lived together and had two sons.

But Jason was not content. Even though Medea had helped him win the Golden Fleece, saved his life multiple times, and even betrayed her own family to be with him, he began to want more power and prestige.

Jason soon betrayed Medea in the worst possible way—he decided to marry another woman. The woman was Glauce, the daughter of the king of Corinth. By marrying her, Jason hoped to secure a royal title and a better future.

When Medea learned about Jason's betrayal, she was heartbroken and furious. She had given up everything for him. And this was how he decided to repay her?

The king of Corinth worried that Medea might seek revenge and ordered her to leave the city immediately. Medea begged for just one more day before she was to leave forever. The king decided to be kind and agreed.

Medea sent a beautiful golden robe and crown to Jason's new bride. Glauce was delighted by the gift and put them on immediately.

But Medea's gift was cursed. The moment Glauce wore the robe and crown, they burst into flames, burning her alive. When her father tried to save her, he was caught in the deadly magic and died in the fire.

And Medea's revenge did not stop there. She knew that the greatest pain she could inflict on Jason was to take away the thing he loved most: his own children. In a shocking and tragic act, Medea killed their two sons, ensuring that Jason's bloodline would end.

When Jason arrived, it was too late. His bride was dead, and his children were gone. Medea fled the city in a chariot pulled by dragons. She traveled to Athens, where she was given refuge by King Aegeus (the father of the legendary hero Theseus).

Jason's broken vow to Medea angered Hera. She withdrew her support from him. As the years passed, he lost everything. In the end, Jason died a lonely and homeless old man. One night, as he was sleeping under the stern of the rotting *Argo*, the stern broke off. Jason was squashed to death.

Chapter 7 Activity

Can you find the words listed below?

WORD LIST

- Jason
- Argonauts
- Fleece
- Heracles
- Medea
- Colchis
- Eros
- Iolcus
- Pelias
- Dragon

J	A	S	O	N	P	R	L	M	A
A	B	C	F	L	E	E	C	E	R
K	I	N	P	Z	L	X	Y	D	G
C	O	L	C	H	I	S	T	E	O
D	L	B	F	V	A	W	L	A	N
R	C	E	R	O	S	G	K	I	A
A	U	T	L	X	E	F	Z	M	U
G	S	R	P	N	V	D	O	S	T
O	S	H	E	R	A	C	L	E	S
N	U	M	R	I	E	P	K	T	A

Chapter 8: The Trojan War

One of the most popular stories of ancient Greece is a war in a city named Troy. It is a *saga* (story) with many heroes. Scholars once thought it was complete fiction. Over time, even the location of Troy was forgotten.

Heinrich Schliemann's Quest for Troy

Do you have a favorite story? In the 1800s, a boy named Heinrich Schliemann was growing up in Germany. His favorite book was the *Iliad*. It was written by a famous Greek poet called Homer. Homer composed the *Iliad* around the 8th century BCE.

Heinrich was fascinated by the story of the ancient Trojan War. It is said he carried the book in his pocket wherever he went. He read it so many times that he could recite long pieces of the text.

Heinrich was sure the legend was based on real events. He worked hard as a grown-up and made lots of money. He was determined to find the city of Troy one day.

Finding Troy

When Heinrich came to the small village of Hissarlik (*hee-sar-lick*) near the west coast of Turkey, he met a British gentleman named Frank Calvert. Frank also thought they were near the site of Troy.

Heinrich got a team together. They started *excavating* (digging out) the large earthen mound. They immediately found signs of cities built on top of each other. The oldest city was at the bottom. Heinrich was sure this was Homer's

Troy. Today, we know that he was wrong. There are nine ruined cities. Homer's Troy was the seventh city from the bottom.

Heinrich's most important find was beautiful jewelry. He gave the jewelry to his Greek wife, Sophia. He told the newspapers that he had found Troy and the jewels of Priam (*prai-uhm*). Priam is thought to have been the king of Troy at the time of the Trojan War.

Can you imagine discovering such a fascinating treasure?

Sophia Schliemann with the gold jewelry her husband found at Troy.[24]

Cause of the Trojan War

Homer's poem starts during the tenth year of the war. The war was started by the kings of Achaea (*ah-kee-yah*). Achaea (Greece) was not a unified country at this time. However, the leaders of the city-states came together to attack Troy.

The Greeks attacked Troy to get the Spartan queen back. Paris, a handsome young prince from Troy, had abducted Helen from the palace of King Menelaus (*meh-nuh-lay-uhs*) of Sparta. Sparta was a Greek city-state.

There is a much larger story behind why the Trojan War started. One myth states that Zeus was concerned about the large number of people on the earth. He caused the Trojan War to reduce their number and to get rid of the many demigods.

Helen of Troy.[25]

Another myth is that the goddess of *discord* (argument), Eris (*uh-ris*), was upset. She was not invited to the wedding feast of the goddess Thetis because she always caused trouble.

Eris went to the feast anyway. She brought a beautiful golden apple as a gift. The gift had an inscription that stated it was "for the fairest." Three goddesses—Athena, Hera, and Aphrodite—each claimed the apple. They argued over it for more than a year!

In the end, they agreed to let a human be the judge. They chose Prince Paris of Troy. The *naïve* (inexperienced) young prince chose Aphrodite, the goddess of love and beauty. She had promised to make the most beautiful woman in the world fall in love with him.

Paris was visiting King Menelaus at the time. Aphrodite did not care that the most beautiful woman was already married or that the situation could cause a war. Helen fell in love with Paris. She sailed away with him to Troy.

King Menelaus called all the Greek kings together. They decided to bring Helen back from Troy. They also wanted to punish the Trojans for their betrayal.

The Siege of Troy

The city of Troy was heavily fortified. When the Greeks arrived, they saw the only way to win was to besiege the city until the Trojans surrendered. This siege would last ten long years.

A *siege* is when an army encamps around the position of its enemies. They block anyone from entering or exiting. It usually ends with the enemy surrendering because they run out of food and water.

Achilles and Ajax play a board game
while there is a pause in the battle.[26]

Achilles (*uh-ki-lees*) and King Agamemnon (*a-guh-mem-naan*) were chosen to lead the attack on Troy. Many great heroes of ancient Greece joined the expedition.

Hera, Athena, and Poseidon helped the Greeks. Apollo, Aphrodite, and Ares sided with the Trojans. Zeus, the king of the gods, tried to stay neutral but secretly had his own plans.

> Agamemnon was the brother of King Menelaus. He was the king of Mycenae.

After almost ten years, the people and the soldiers were tired of the fighting. The Greek kings and their armies wanted to return home to their families. They had tried everything, but they could not get into Troy. The Achaeans (Greeks) were even getting irritated with each other.

Sickness had broken out in the Greek camp. Many died. They did not know it was the gods interfering once again. Apollo sent a pandemic to punish the Greeks after they had taken two beautiful girls from a nearby village. One was the daughter of a priest of Apollo. The local seer told the famed hero Achilles that Apollo would only bring healing to the Greek camp if Agamemnon gave her back to her father.

Achilles and Agamemnon Fall Out

Agamemnon refused to give the girl back. All of the Greek kings pleaded with him. When he finally agreed, he demanded compensation.

Achilles and Agamemnon argue.[27]

Achilles, the greatest warrior of the Greeks, was furious. He had just found out that Agamemnon planned to take away his prize—a young woman he had gained during the war—just to prove his power. Achilles felt insulted. After all, he had fought hard in the war. Agamemnon should not be able to take away what was his.

In his rage, Achilles almost drew his sword to strike Agamemnon down. But just before he could, Athena appeared before him. She told him, "If you harm Agamemnon now, you will lose your honor. Be patient. One day, you will have your revenge."

Achilles lowered his sword but stated he would not fight for the Greeks anymore. He turned his back on the war and stormed away from the battlefield. He went to the shore and prayed to his mother, Thetis, a sea goddess. He begged her to ask Zeus to punish the Greeks by allowing the Trojans to win the war for a while so they would realize how much they needed him.

Thetis went to Zeus. Although he knew this request would cause conflict among the gods, he agreed. He sent a false dream to Agamemnon, making him believe that the Greeks would win if they attacked the Trojans. This led to a new battle, but without Achilles and his warriors, the Greeks began to struggle.

Meanwhile, in Troy, the mighty warrior Prince Hector of Troy, the leader of the Trojan army, prepared for battle. Hector was the Greeks' greatest challenge, and it seemed no Greek could stop him.

Without Achilles, the Greeks were vulnerable. The Trojans began pushing them back toward their ships. The fate of the war hung in the balance. Achilles would soon be forced to decide whether to stay in his tent or return to battle.

As the battle raged, the gods took sides once again. Apollo and Ares helped the Trojans. Athena and Hera did their best to support the Greeks. But no matter how hard the Greeks fought, they could not stop Hector and his warriors.

Things became even worse when Hector and the Trojans broke through the Greek defenses and set fire to their ships. If the Greek ships were destroyed, there would be no way for them to escape. The war would be lost.

One Greek could not stand by watching his friends suffer. Patroclus, Achilles's best friend, rushed to Achilles's tent. He begged him to return to battle, but Achilles refused. He was still angry at King Agamemnon.

"If you won't fight," Patroclus said, "then at least let me wear your armor! The Trojans fear you. If they think you have returned, they will retreat."

Achilles agreed but warned his friend. "Scare them, but do not chase them all the way to the gates of Troy. That is my fight, not yours."

Patroclus dressed in Achilles's armor and led his men into battle. The Trojans thought Achilles had returned. They panicked and ran. Patroclus fought bravely. He even killed a great Trojan warrior. However, in his excitement, he forgot Achilles's warning. He chased the Trojans too far. He went all the way to the gates of Troy.

Hector confronted him. The two warriors fought fiercely, but Hector struck Patroclus down.

When Achilles heard that Patroclus was dead, he was devastated. He no longer cared about his argument with Agamemnon. All he wanted was revenge.

His mother saw his grief and promised to have the god Hephaestus forge him a new suit of armor and a mighty shield. The next day, Achilles stormed onto the battlefield. He was ready to make Hector pay for his friend's death.

The Trojans were scared when they saw him. They knew he would not stop until Hector was dead.

Achilles finally found Hector at the city gates. Hector ran around the city, and Achilles chased him. In the fourth lap around the city, Zeus tipped his scale in favor of Achilles. He killed Hector. Then, he dragged Hector's body with his chariot. This was a sign of disrespect in ancient times. Many days later, King Priam went to the Greeks' camp to get his son's body. Achilles let him take the body with him.

Achilles dragging Hector's dead body behind his chariot.[28]

Achilles arranged a big funeral for Patroclus. The Greeks built a huge funeral pyre to burn his body. The next day, they collected the bones and buried them in a new tomb. Achilles was promised that he would be buried next to Patroclus when his time came.

Even though Homer's account in the *Iliad* ends here, the war still dragged on. Another one of Homer's epic poems, the *Odyssey*, talks about the end of the war.

You may recall that Achilles was the son of a human father and the goddess Thetis. This means he was mortal. When he was an infant, his mother dipped him into the River Styx to make his mortal parts immortal. She held him by his heel. This heel was his only vulnerable part.

Paris, Hector's brother, killed Achilles. His arrow was guided by Apollo, and it hit Achilles in his heel. He was mortally wounded and died.

Fun Fact

> You may have heard the term "Achilles's heel" before. That term comes from this story. It means a weak or vulnerable point.

Paris was killed by a Greek arrow. Helen married one of Paris's brothers. She later betrayed this brother so she could return to Sparta with Menelaus.

The Trojan Horse

But how did the Greeks overcome the Trojans? That is quite an interesting story. The Greeks were advised by a prophetess that they needed three things to win the war.

They needed a descendant of Achilles to join them. They also needed a descendant of Heracles. Thirdly, they would only get into Troy by using deception.

Replica of the Trojan Horse in Turkey.[29]

The Greeks managed the first two easily, but they were stumped on how to trick the Trojans. A ruler named Odysseus suggested they could build a very large statue of a horse. Greek soldiers could then hide inside it. The rest of the Greeks must sail away, pretending to leave. However, they would hide their ships behind a nearby island.

Fun Fact

" Odysseus was the king of Ithaca. His story was so popular among the Greeks that Homer wrote a whole book about him. "

The wooden horse intrigued the Trojans the next day when they came out to do battle. They wondered what this enormous statue could mean. And where were all the Greeks? Could this horse be a gift for all that death and hardship?

One Greek remained behind. He complained that everyone had left him. He also insisted that the horse was meant to be a present. The Trojans never assumed that this Greek would light a fire later that night. That fire would tell the Greeks on the nearby island that it was time to attack.

The Trojans held a feast to celebrate. Almost everyone went to bed tired and drunk.

The burning of Troy.[30]

During the night, the captured Greek let the soldiers out through a trapdoor in the horse. They opened the gates of Troy. And then they attacked. Since the Trojans were sleeping, the Greeks had an advantage.

The Trojans were massacred in the battle, and Troy was burned to the ground. Only a few Trojans got away. One Trojan who escaped was a hero named Aeneas. A Roman poet named Virgil wrote about Aeneas's story in the *Aeneid*. The Romans believed Aeneas was the father of their nation.

Chapter 8 Activity

Mark which statement is true and which is false.

	Statement	True	False
1	Homer wrote a comic book about the Trojan War		
2	Sophia Schliemann showed Heinrich Schliemann the location of Troy		
3	The ancient Greeks were called the Achaeans by Homer		
4	The Turkish village where Troy was rediscovered is Hissarlik		
5	The Trojan War lasted a hundred years		
6	Hector was the best and bravest of the Trojan soldiers		
7	Achilles was the best and bravest of the Greek soldiers		
8	Odysseus was the leader of the Trojan troops		
9	The Greeks used a large wooden horse to trick the Trojans		
10	The Greeks won the Trojan War		

Activity Solutions

Chapter 1

Chapter 2

1. c) Titans;
2. a) Gaia
3. b) Cronos
4. c) Rhea
5. a) Swallowed them
6. c) On the island of Crete
7. c) Zeus
8. c) Titanomachy
9. c) Zeus
10. b) Poseidon

Chapter 3

ACROSS

2. Eagle
4. Liver
6. Prometheus

DOWN

1. Flood
2. Athena
5. Mud

10. Men
11. Stones
13. Ship
14. Destroy

6. Pandora
7. Ox
8. Hope
9. Feast
12. Fire

Chapter 4

1. c. Demigod
3. c. Hera
5. c. Lion
7. c. White
9. c. Dog

2. c. Zeus
4. b. Twelve
6. c. Nine
8. c. Rivers
10. b. Slingshot

Chapter 6

1. Andromeda
3. Atlas
5. Athena
7. Gorgons
9. Danae

2. Cassiopeia
4. Cetus
6. Medusa
8. Dictys
10. Pegasus

Chapter 7

J	A	S	O	N	P		M	A	
			F	L	E	E	C	E	R
	I				L			D	G
C	O	L	C	H	I	S		E	O
D	L				A			A	N
R	C	E	R	O	S				A
A	U								U
G	S								T
O	S	H	E	R	A	C	L	E	S
N									

Chapter 8

	Statement	True	False
1	Homer wrote a comic book about the Trojan War		✓
2	Sophia Schliemann showed Heinrich Schliemann the location of Troy		✓
3	The ancient Greeks were called the Achaeans by Homer	✓	
4	The Turkish village where Troy was rediscovered is Hissarlik	✓	
5	The Trojan War lasted a hundred years		✓
6	Hector was the best and bravest of the Trojan soldiers	✓	
7	Achilles was the best and bravest of the Greek soldiers	✓	
8	Odysseus was the leader of the Trojan troops		✓
9	The Greeks used a large wooden horse to trick the Trojans	✓	
10	The Greeks won the Trojan War	✓	

If you want to learn more about tons of other exciting historical periods, check out our other books!

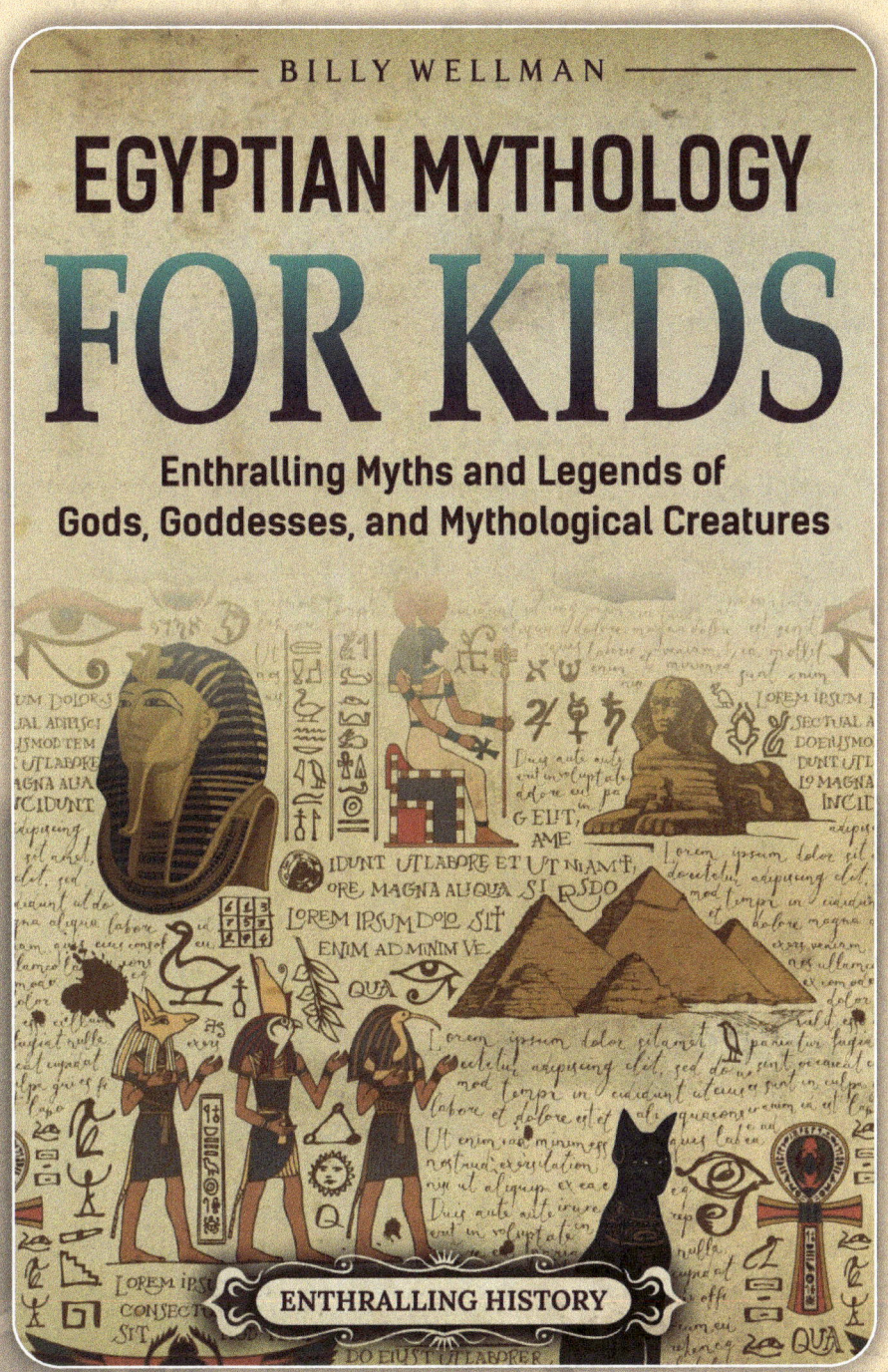

Bibliography

*Tip: If you would like to *hear* how to say some of the difficult names, you may visit the following website, fill in the word, and listen to the pronunciation: https://www.howtopronounce.com

** If you would like to read more about the hero Odysseus, you can read a full summary of Homer's *Odyssey* online at

https://www.litcharts.com/lit/the-odyssey/book-1
https://www.litcharts.com/lit/the-iliad/
https://www.sparknotes.com/lit/odyssey/section7/
http://www.stoa.org/hopper/text.jsp?doc=Stoa:text:2003.01.0004:account=5
https://www.bbc.co.uk/teach/class-clips-video/ks2-history-ancient-greece-creation-myth-the-olympians/zf86p4j
https://www.livescience.com/38191-ancient-troy.html#section-troy-today
https://www.greekmyths-greekmythology.com/
https://www.thoughtco.com/flood-myth-of-deucalion-and-pyrrha-119917
141 Nemean Lion Facts: Story From The Greek Mythology You Should Know | Kidadl
https://www.perseus.tufts.edu/Heracles/boar.html
http://classics.mit.edu/Plutarch/theseus.html
https://web.archive.org/web/20150924111536/
https://www.perseus.tufts.edu/hopper/text?doc=Perseus:text:1999.04.0104:entry=theseus-bio-1
Ancient Greece UNIT for Teachers (mrdonn.org)

Videos:
The Trojan Horse | TRADITIONAL STORY | Classic Story for kids | Fairy Tales | BIGBOX #fairytales - YouTube
Greek Mythology for Kids | What is mythology? Learn all about Greek mythology - YouTube
Greek Mythology for Kids | Greek Gods and Goddesses | Twinkl USA - YouTube
A Child's Introduction to Greek Mythology (Excerpts) - YouTube
Pandora's Box | The Greek Myth of Pandora and Her Box | Greek Mythology Story - YouTube

Images Sources

[1] Mearone, FAL, via Wikimedia Commons;
https://commons.wikimedia.org/wiki/File:GAIA_by_mearone.jpg
[2] Roscher W. H., CC0, via Wikimedia Commons;
https://commons.wikimedia.org/wiki/File:Gaia_Kourotrophos_Roscher.jpg
[3] DerekGil, CC BY-SA 4.0 <https://creativecommons.org/licenses/by-sa/4.0>, via Wikimedia Commons;
https://commons.wikimedia.org/wiki/File:Estatua_de_Urano,_Fuente_de_Trevi,_Roma.jpg
[4] GFreihalter, CC BY-SA 3.0 <https://creativecommons.org/licenses/by-sa/3.0>, via Wikimedia Commons;
https://commons.wikimedia.org/wiki/File:Ellingen_Deutschordensschloss_414.jpg
[5] George Shuklin, CC BY-SA 3.0 <http://creativecommons.org/licenses/by-sa/3.0/>, via Wikimedia Commons;
[6] https://commons.wikimedia.org/wiki/File:J-B_de_Champaigne_Hercule_mourant.jpg
[7] https://commons.wikimedia.org/wiki/File:Heinrich_fueger_1817_prometheus_brings_fire_to_mankind.jpg
[8] https://commons.wikimedia.org/w/index.php?curid=10827197
[9] https://commons.wikimedia.org/wiki/File:Peter_Paul_Rubens_-_Deucalion_and_Pyrrha,_1636.jpg
[10] https://commons.wikimedia.org/wiki/File:Herakles_snake_Musei_Capitolini_MC247.jpg
[11] https://commons.wikimedia.org/wiki/File:H%C3%A9rakl%C3%A9sz_H%C3%BCdra_Iolaosz.png
[12] J. M. Fëlix Magdalena, CC BY-SA 4.0 <https://creativecommons.org/licenses/by-sa/4.0>, via Wikimedia Commons
https://commons.wikimedia.org/wiki/File:Lucha_de_Heracles_con_el_toro_de_Creta.jpg
[13] https://commons.wikimedia.org/wiki/File:GardenHesperides_BurneJones.jpg
[14] https://commons.wikimedia.org/wiki/File:Laurent_de_la_La_Hyre_002.jpg
[15] https://commons.wikimedia.org/wiki/File:Theseus_and_the_Minotaur.gif
[16] Livioandronico2013, CC BY-SA 4.0 <https://creativecommons.org/licenses/by-sa/4.0>, via Wikimedia Commons;
https://commons.wikimedia.org/wiki/File:Theseus_slaying_the_Minotaur.jpg
[17] https://commons.wikimedia.org/wiki/File:JohnWilliamWaterhouse-Dana%C3%AB(1892).jpg

[18] Tantrik71, CC BY-SA 3.0 <https://creativecommons.org/licenses/by-sa/3.0>, via Wikimedia Commons; https://commons.wikimedia.org/wiki/File:%D0%9F%D0%B5%D1%80%D1%81%D0%B5%D0%B9_%D1%81_%D0%B3%D0%BE%D0%BB%D0%BE%D0%B2%D0%BE%D0%B9_%D0%9C%D0%B5%D0%B4%D1%83%D0%B7%D1%8B.jpg

[19] Montrealais, CC BY 3.0 <https://creativecommons.org/licenses/by/3.0>, via Wikimedia Commons; https://commons.wikimedia.org/wiki/File:Perseus_and_andromeda_amphora.jpg

[20] Perseus constellation PP3 map PL.jpg:Blueshade at pl.wikipediaderivative work: Olalancette, CC BY-SA 3.0; http://creativecommons.org/licenses/by-sa/3.0/>, via Wikimedia Commons https://commons.wikimedia.org/wiki/File:Perseus_constellation_PP3_map_FR.jpg

[21] Biagio d'Antonio, CC0, via Wikimedia Commons; https://commons.wikimedia.org/wiki/File:Scenes_from_the_Story_of_the_Argonauts_MET_DP164779.jpg

[22] https://commons.wikimedia.org/wiki/File:Constantine_Volanakis_Argo.jpg

[23] ; https://commons.wikimedia.org/wiki/File:Erasmus_Quellinus_(II)-_Jason_with_the_Golden_Fleece,_1630.jpg

[24] https://commons.wikimedia.org/wiki/File:Sophia_Schliemann_wearing_Treasure_A,_Troy.jpg

[25] https://commons.wikimedia.org/wiki/File:Helen_of_Troy.jpg

[26] Sailko, CC BY-SA 3.0 <https://creativecommons.org/licenses/by-sa/3.0>, via Wikimedia Commons; https://commons.wikimedia.org/wiki/File:Exekias,_anfora_con_achille_e_aiace_che_giocano_a_dai,_castore_e_polluce,_da_vulci,_540-30_ac_ca._03.JPG

[27] https://commons.wikimedia.org/wiki/File:Tischbein_Joh._Hr._d._%C3%84._Achilles%27_Dispute_with_Agamemnon@Kunsthalle_Hamburg.JPG

[28] https://commons.wikimedia.org/wiki/File:Triumph_of_Achilles_in_Corfu_Achilleion.jpg

[29] Fredrik Posse, Copyrighted free use, via Wikimedia Commons; https://commons.wikimedia.org/wiki/File:Trojan_horse_in_Canakkale,_Turkey.jpg

[30] https://commons.wikimedia.org/wiki/File:J_G_Trautmann_Das_brennende_Troja.jpg

www.ingramcontent.com/pod-product-compliance
Lightning Source LLC
Chambersburg PA
CBHW072102050526
44107CB00099B/384